FAMILY MATTERS

CARD GAMES

FAMILY MATTERS

CARD GAMES

MICHAEL JOHNSTONE

WARD LOCK

First published in Great Britain in 1988
by Ward Lock Limited, Villiers House, 41–47 Strand,
London WC2N 5JE, a Cassell Company.

Reprinted 1990, 1991

Text set in Sabon 10½pt
by Columns of Reading
Printed and bound in Great Britain
Collins Manufacturing, Glasgow

British Library Cataloguing in Publication Data
Johnstone, Michael
    Card games.
    1. Cards
    I. Title
    795.4   GV1243
    ISBN 0–7063–6635–2

CONTENTS

INTRODUCTION

Card games are probably the most widespread of all forms of indoor entertainment and their origin goes back to the Middle Ages, if not earlier. By the fifteenth century cards were being used in Italy and soon became popular all over Europe.

The earliest Italian cards were the tarot cards which were used for the game *tarocchi*. From these came the 52-card English and French packs, the 48-card Spanish pack and the 32-card German pack. Tarot cards are still used today to tell fortunes and give character readings.

The four suits with which we are familiar, spades, hearts, diamonds and clubs, originated in France. Other countries have their own. The suits that we call diamonds and clubs are represented by bells and acorns in Germany and Switzerland, and coins and swords in Italy and Spain. Spades and hearts are flowers and shields in Switzerland, leaves and hearts in Germany and batons and cups in Spain and Italy. The characters on our court cards are still depicted wearing clothes in the style worn by courtiers in medieval France.

There are a wide range of card games, some with conventions so complex that whole books have been written to explain them, while others are so simple that young children can play and enjoy them. There are card games for four or more players, games for three, games for two, and games of Patience – the player against the pack, which can be so diabolically frustrating that the player comes to understand that not for nothing have playing cards come to be known as the Devil's picture-book.

WORDS IN THE WORLD
OF CARDS

Ace High: in games where the ace is high it scores above the king. In such games the two is the lowest card.

Ace Low: in some games the ace scores below the two and the king is the highest scoring card.

Bid: to declare before play how many tricks you expect to take.

Corner marks: all cards are marked with their rank and suit in the corners. Court cards are marked A for ace, K for king, Q for queen and J for jack (or knave).

Court Cards: the picture cards in each suit.

Cutting the Cards: each player lifts a block of cards off the pack which is then placed face down in the centre of the table. Everyone looks at the bottom card of his block, and the player who cuts the highest card wins.

Deal: the dealer holds the cards face down, and distributes them one at a time face down onto the table in front of each player including himself. The deal should be a clockwise direction.

Discard: when a player is unable to follow suit and has no trump cards, he plays a card from another suit, i.e. he discards.

Follow Suit: in most card games players have to follow suit by playing a card of the same suit as the one played at the start of the round.

Hand: the cards held by a player.

Honours: the ace, king, queen and jack of trumps.

Meld: a matched set of three or more of a kind or a sequence of three or more of the same suit in consecutive order or rank.

Misere: pronounced 'miz-air', this is a declaration by

a player that he does not expect to take any tricks.

Overtrump: to play a higher trump card than has already been played in a round.

Pack: the complete set of 52 cards. Also called the deck, especially in the United States.

Packet: a pile of cards.

Pass: to miss a turn or to refuse to bid.

Pips: the number of a suit that appears on the card: e.g. the eight value card has eight pips.

Plain (or *Side) Suit:* a suit other than the trump suit.

Rank: the order of the cards ranging from two to the ace if aces are high, or from ace to king if aces are low.

Revoke (or *Renege):* to fail to follow suit when able to do so.

Rubber: a series of games, especially in bridge or whist.

Shuffle: to mix the cards.

Singleton: an original holding of a single card in a suit.

School: the collective noun for a group of gambling card players.

Stock: the pile of cards left in the middle. In some card games players draw new cards from the stock.

Talon: cards in games of patience in one or more packets for use later in the same deal.

Trick: the set of cards (one from each player) played in one round, usually taken by whoever plays the highest card of the suit led or the highest trump.

Trumps: cards of a chosen suit that outrank all the other suits for the duration of a deal or game.

Void: having no cards of a specified suit.

Yarborough: a hand of thirteen cards in which no card is higher than a nine.

GAMES OF PATIENCE

In *Othello*, Iago says 'How poor are they that have not patience!' He was referring to the virtue rather than to any card game, but his words could easily be applied to anyone who has not discovered the joys of a game or two of Patience.

There are over 500 varieties of the game, some requiring skill, others requiring nothing but luck. Many are based on the principle of building up the pack in descending or ascending sequence on specific foundation cards. If he or she succeeds, the player defeats what English actress Margaret Rutherford, who was a great Patience player, described as 'an invisible opponent, yet a comrade.'

• • • • •

Before describing the rules and methods of play of several games of Patience there are some words that must be explained.

Available cards are those that are not blocked by other cards, that is they can be used in accordance with the particular rules of a particular game.

Foundation cards are the cards on which the Patience is built: they are usually aces and kings.

Lanes are empty spaces in the tableau which have been formed by the removal of an entire row of cards.

Marriage is the placing of a card of the same suit on the next one above it or below it in value.

Sequences are regular successions of cards ascending from ace to king or descending from king to ace. Sequences need not be of one suit.

Suitable cards are those whose value and suit fit them to be played or placed in the tableau.

Tableau is the display of cards on the table.

ROUND THE CLOCK

Margaret Rutherford's invisible adversary usually wins at this simple game which demands no skill. But when he wins, the player feels a sense of achievement out of all proportion to the victory.

Shuffle a pack of cards and lay them one at a time in clock formation on the card table. The first card goes at 'one', the second at 'two' and so on until the thirteenth card which goes in the centre. Start at 'one' again with the fourteenth card and continue round and round until the last card is put on top of the other three in the middle of the clock. Tidy-minded people usually neaten the thirteen piles, at least for the first two or three rounds after which even they are so desperate to beat the clock that they start to play as soon as the last card has been put into position in the tableau.

Play starts by picking up the top card from the central packet. It is put on the outside of its partner packet: so, if an ace is the first card drawn it is put outside the circle of cards alongside 'one'. A knave goes alongside the 'eleven' packet and a queen goes at 'twelve'. The top card is removed from that packet and placed where it belongs and so on until the packets of face-down cards in the inner circle are getting fewer and fewer and there are more and more cards in the upturned packets.

BUT if the card drawn is a king, it goes alongside the central packet and the next card is drawn from that pile. So when three kings have been turned up, the central pile is empty, and if the last king is turned up before all the outer, upturned piles have been completed the player loses, for there will be no cards left in the centre from which to draw.

The odds on getting out are heavily against the player, but that doesn't stop addicts trying again, and again, and again . . .

ROUND THE CLOCK

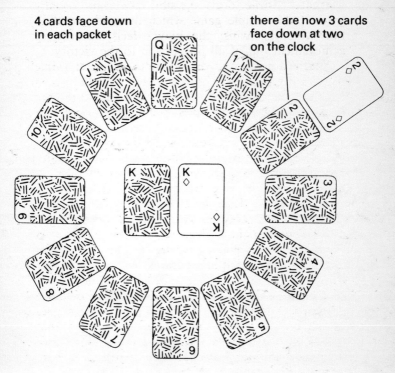

4 cards face down in each packet

there are now 3 cards face down at two on the clock

The first card drawn from the centre packet was a two. It has been placed at two on the clock and the top card from the packet has been played. Unfortunately it was a king, so it was placed alongside the centre packet from which the next card has to be drawn, reducing the centre packet to two cards.

SEVEN UP

This game is also known as Klondike and Canfield, the latter because it is thought to have been devised by a nineteenth-century casino owner, Richard Canfield.

Deal a row of seven cards face down from a 52-card pack. Now deal a card face down on top of the card second from the left, covering the one beneath it, and continue to add one card face down on the cards to the right. Now do the same starting with the card third from the left, then fourth until you have seven packets, one card on the left hand one, two on the next, three on the next . . . and seven on the final one. Turn over the top cards of each packet.

The aim is to get the aces out, lay them along the top and use them as foundation cards to build up suits from ace to king.

If any aces are showing, move them to the top and turn over the next card down. If any twos of the same suit as revealed aces are showing, add them to the foundation.

Now build up sequences using the revealed cards in each packet as the foundations for sequences of cards in descending order of alternate colours. e.g. black eight on red nine: sequences can be moved onto appropriate foundation cards. The top card of each packet should always be face up.

Once you have made all possible moves, take the stock and count out a batch of three. Turn the batch face up on the table. If the top card can be used in any of the alternate colour sequences or in the foundation suits above, put it in position. If the second card can be similarly used, do so. And again if the last card can be positioned on the table. You can't use the second card unless you can play the top one.

When you can no longer play, turn over another three card batch and play them in the same way. The stock must not be shuffled and must only be used in three card batches.

You can fill up empty lanes by moving the

upturned cards in the lane on its right, across. Turn over the next card in this pile as the foundation for a new sequence. Only the bottom card of each lane on the tableau can be moved up to the foundations. When *all* the cards are married in ascending order, the game is over: but there is no guarantee that the cards will come out each time.

LOVELY LUCY

Deal a pack of cards into packets of three so that you have seventeen packets and one single card. Arrange them in rows, face up: six packets in the top row, five packets underneath them, four in the next row and in the fourth row have two packets of three on the outside with the single card in the middle of them. Fan the cards in each packet.

Only the right-hand card in each packet can be played. Only when it is played is the next card released. The aim of the game is to marry the suits in ascending order, ace to king, in the space between the bottom row of two packets and the single card and the edge of the table.

Once you have placed the tableau take out any available aces, then suitable twos, threes and so on until you have made all possible moves.

The end card of each fan can be moved to the end of another fan if it is the card below it in the same suit. This releases more cards for play. When all available cards have been played, the remaining cards in the tableau are shuffled and redealt into packets of three, laid face up into a new tableau which will have fewer packets than the original. The extra one or two cards are also displayed face up and the game begins again until all possble cards have been played.

One more shuffle and tableau is allowed. If, when all possible cards have been played from the tableau, the four suits have not been completed, our old friend, the Invisible Adversary has won.

LOVELY LUCY
 A section of the tableau at the start of the game.

 Possible moves are:
  1. Remove HA to its foundation.
  2. H5 on to H6.
  3. H6 and H5 on to H7.
  4. H7, H6, and H5 on to H8.
  5. DA to its foundation.

THE ZODIAC

Deal eight cards from two packs in a horizontal row: this is the Equator. Now deal a surrounding circle of twenty-four cards: this is the Zodiac.

 Foundations, which are not formed until the end of the game, are to consist of the four aces and four kings of different suits. Aces ascend in married sequence to kings and kings descend in married sequence to aces.

Once the tableau has been placed, play the cards in the pack one by one hoping to marry cards from the pack with cards in the Zodiac. Marriages can be made in ascending or descending order and the same packet can contain both. Marriages can be made in the Zodiac with cards from the Equator, but not vice versa. Inter-Zodiac marriages and inter-Equator marriages are not permitted. Gaps that are created are filled with cards from the pack.

Deal the cards in the usual way. Cards not required for marrying or for refilling spaces form the talon. This is redealt as often as need be until all the cards are either in the Zodiac or the Equator.

If you succeed in placing all the cards, begin to form the eight foundations, marrying cards in accordance with the rules to reveal the cards necessary for the foundation.

SIR TOMMY

After the intricacies of The Zodiac, it is a relief to come to one of the simplest games of Patience, which is also one of the oldest, hence its other name, Old Patience.

The aim of the game is to find the four aces and use them as the foundation cards to create four packets of thirteen cards each, ace to king. The sequences are not in suit.

With the pack face down, deal the top card and turn it face upwards on the table. As more cards are dealt, create four packets. You can put cards on any pile you like.

When the aces are dealt, line them up side by side above the four packets. When you have an ace, you need a two to continue the sequence, then a three and so on. Cards can be placed on foundations immediately they are dealt from the pack, but cards in the lines that are needed to continue the sequence cannot be used until they are released by the card above it being played. If by playing a card on a foundation, you lose a packet, you can create a new one from the pack or by moving over cards from another packet: this can be helpful in unblocking required cards.

BLOCKADE

The foundation cards in Blockade are the eight aces from two packs of cards. Foundations must follow suit.

Deal out twelve cards in a horizontal line. Any aces that appear can be played straight away. No other card can be played until the line is complete.

When the twelve cards are placed, make any marriages in descending sequence, carefully ensuring that top cards are placed exactly over the ones

BLOCKADE

An ace was dealt in the setting out of the tableau and was immediately played to foundation. On this tableau the following marriages can be made before the next line is laid out.

   1. The five of spades on to the six of spades.
   2. The four of hearts on to the five of hearts.
   3. The two of spades on to the ace.

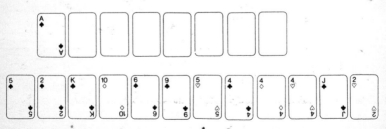

beneath. This avoids confusion.

Any vacancies that are caused must be refilled immediately from the pack. When all possible plays and marriages have been made, deal out another row of twelve cards underneath the first. Again, only aces may be played as they appear. When it is complete play, marry and refill spaces as before.

Continue to deal out successive rows until there are no more cards left in the pack, playing, marrying and refilling spaces.

Each new row blocks the row above it. It is only when a vacancy is created in the bottom row, that you can play the card on top of the packet immediately above.

Vacancies created in superior rows must be filled from the pack before vacancies in the bottom line are filled.

Before the next line is laid out, the tableau is thus:

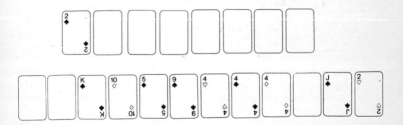

Remember that vacancies in higher rows should be filled first.

LE CADRAN

Two packs of cards are needed to play Le Cadran (French for dial or face). There are only two rules: no card can be used that has another below it (i.e. only cards in the lowest row are available for play; a card in any row is only released by the removal of those below it), and the foundations must follow suit.

Deal out from left to right four rows of ten cards. Any aces in the bottom row should be removed and used as foundation cards. Any twos now available for marriage can now be removed from the lines and put on top of the relevant aces: then threes and so on until none of the available cards can be played.

LE CADRAN

The first move to make on this tableau is to remove the ace of spades from the bottom row to its allotted foundation. The four of clubs is now available for play and could be played on the five of clubs next to it, releasing the ace of clubs which can be moved to its foundation. The two of clubs can be played on the ace, now releasing the three of spades . . . and so on.

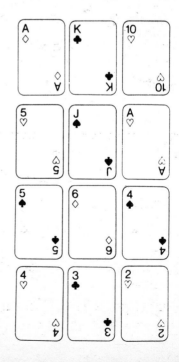

At the same time as building married foundations in ascending order out of the tableau, marriages are created in descending order within the tableau, always subject to the rules.

When all possible moves have been made, the rest of the cards are turned over one by one. They can be played either on the foundations or on the married sequences in the tableau.

If when making moves, a vacancy is created in the top line, it can be filled by moving up any available card from the tableau or using a card in the talon. Cards that cannot be played are laid aside in the talon. There is no redeal.

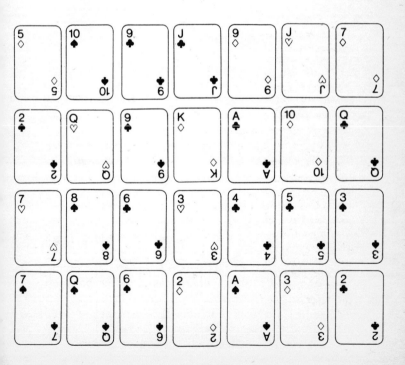

LE PARTERRE

Deal six packets of six cards dealt together and spread them out so that they are all visible. These cards are *Le Parterre* (the flowerbed). The remaining sixteen cards are *Le Bouquet*.

The aces are the foundation cards. Foundations must follow suit in ascending order, but cards placed in sequence on the *Parterre* need not follow suit.

Spread the *Bouquet* out in front of you, so that you can see all the cards.

Cards are released for the foundation packets by moving the cards on top of them to other packets within the *Parterre* or from the *Bouquet* to the *Parterre*. This is done by placing cards in descending sequences in the *Parterre* transferring them as often as you like. Cards can placed from the *Bouquet* in the same way, but cannot be returned from the *Parterre* to the *Bouquet*.

So, if an ace was the second card down in a packet and the one above it was a four, to release the ace the four has to be put on top of another packet the top card of which is a five. Any card from the *Bouquet* is available.

When a packet is exhausted, you may begin a new one with any of the cards from the *Bouquet* or any available in the *Parterre*. This is just what you want if the top card in another packet is a king. This is a very demanding patience. There is only one deal and cards taken from the *Bouquet* cannot be returned to it. Great care is needed when placing cards in sequence and in playing them. You don't have to do either, in fact it is often better to leave a card that can be played where it is as it may be more use later on in the game.

A modification that makes the game easier is to build up sequences in the *Parterre* in either descending or ascending order.

LE PARTERRE

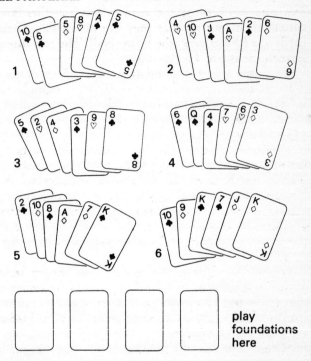

play
foundations
here

The seven of clubs can be taken from Le Bouquet and played on the eight of clubs in Le Parterre on packet three. Now the six of diamonds can be played from packet two on to packet three and the five of clubs on packet one on to the six of diamonds now on packet three. The ace of spades is now released to its foundation and the two of spades now the top card of packet two can be played to its foundation ace. With the king of diamonds the top card of packet six, the only way to release the cards under it for play is to create an empty packet in Le Parterre and move the king over. Cards from Le Bouquet can be played on Le Parterre but once there they may not be taken back to Le Bouquet.

THE EMPRESS OF INDIA

Four packs of cards are needed to play The Empress of India. Take the eight black aces, eight black queens. eight red kings and eight red knaves. Discard all the black queens apart from one queen of clubs. She is the Empress and she sits at the centre of the tableau.

The Empress is guarded by the red knaves: two knaves of hearts stand alongside each other at the top with the other two knaves of hearts to protect her base. Two knaves of diamonds protect her right flank and the other two stand guard on her left side: position them so that the bases of the knaves of diamonds are parallel to the sides of the Empress.

The foundation cards are now placed on the tableau. The black aces, known as the Admirals, are laid out so that two of the club aces are above the topmost knaves of hearts and two below the lower pair of heart knaves. The spade aces are put alongside the diamond knaves, base of ace to top of knave. The red kings, the Generals, are positioned so that the four heart kings sit outside the black aces, i.e. there is one heart king atop the club aces and one heart king beneath the two lower club aces and so on. The four diamond kings sit at 45° to the right angles formed by the red knaves. Aces ascend in married sequences to kings: kings descend in married sequences to aces. Red sequences omit knaves and black ones omit queens.

We now lay out the Army and Navy – four horizontal rows of twelve cards each. The upper two rows (the Army) are composed entirely of red cards: the lower two rows (the Navy) are composed entirely of black cards. They are dealt from the pack at the same time. If two rows of one colour, say red, are complete before the other, all the red cards that turn up before the black rows are complete must be laid aside as a red talon. The same rule applies if the black rows are completed before the red, in which case black cards that are turned up before the red rows are complete, form a black talon.

After all that, you are now ready to play!

The rules are as follows:

1) All cards in the Army and Navy are equally available as long as they are played in pairs of different colours. No card of either colour can be played on a foundation unless a card of the other colour is played at the same time on another foundation.

2) The talon consists of two packets, one red and one black.

3) When cards from the Army and Navy are played on foundations, the vacancies that are created must be immediately refilled with cards of their own colour from the talon. If the relevant packet is exhuasted the vacancy is created from the pack. So if a vacancy occurs in the Army ranks (the red cards) and there is no red packet in the talon, cards are turned over from the pack, black cards being added to the black packet until a red card appears.

4) Cards from the pack cannot be put on their foundations as soon as they appear: they must pass through the Army or Navy.

5) The foundations must follow suit.

The setting out of the tableau and the way the horizontal lines are formed often confuse novices at this game. Think of the pack as recruits for either the Army or the Navy. They have to enlist (be put in a vacancy that occurs in one of the four horizontal rows) before they can join their General or Admiral (the foundations) to defend the Empress.

When the Army and Navy are complete, any available pairs that have been dealt can be played.

THE EMPRESS OF INDIA

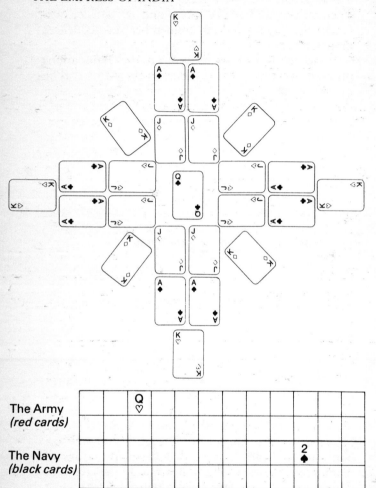

The Army (red cards)		Q ♡									
The Navy (black cards)							2 ♠				

*The first pair, the queen of hearts and the two of
spades, can be played on their foundations. Cards must
go through the ranks before they can be played in pairs
of different colours to their foundations.*

The first pair must be a black two and a red queen. Then either another black two and red queen, or a black three and a red ten (remember red sequences omit knaves).

If no cards can be played on the foundations proceed to pair cards. Any card in the Army can be placed on any card in the Navy and vice versa, but the cards paired in this way cannot be separated and must be played at the same time on their foundations. Vacancies so created must be immediately refilled in accordance with rule 3.

The skill in playing The Empress of India comes from knowing when to make pairings.

When all available cards have been played, proceed to deal out the remainder of the pack. Cards not required to fill vacancies in the Army and Navy are placed in the relevant packet.

There is no redeal.

Beginners find The Empress of India one of the more confusing games of Patience, but once they have mastered the pairings and the way they are placed on their foundations, it is one of the most fascinating of games.

THE SULTAN

You need two packs of cards for this game in which the foundations must follow suit. Remove the eight kings and one ace of hearts and lay them out in three lines of three: in the top line, the ace is placed between the two kings of clubs; in the second line one king of hearts is placed between the kings of diamonds; the other king of hearts is in the centre of the two kings of spades on the bottom line.

The centre king of hearts is The Sultan. The other eight cards are the foundation cards and ascend as follows. On top of each king goes an ace of the same suit, then a two, three and so on: a two of hearts goes on top of the ace at the centre of the top line, then a three, four. . . . As both kings of hearts are foundation cards, if the game works out, The Sultan will be surrounded by a harem of eight concubines.

Now deal four cards, lying sideways, down the left hand side of the tableau, followed by four down the right hand side. These cards are the collective Divan. Play any suitable Divan cards onto the foundation cards.

Now deal the rest of the cards one by one, putting suitable cards on their appropriate foundation packets. Cards that cannot be played are set to one side to form the talon. When it is possible to play a card from the Divan you must replace it immediately with the last card put in the talon, or if there is no talon, with the next card from the pack.

When all the cards in the pack are in a foundation packet, in the Divan or in the talon, shuffle the talon to make a new pack and start again. The talon can only be redealt twice.

THE FOUR CORNERS

As the language of cards is French, this game is properly called *Les Quatres Coins*. Two packs are needed. The rules are straightforward: Once the deal is completed, the uppermost card in each packet is available and can be played on any of the foundations, the cards beneath being released only when the one covering it has been removed.

Deal out two columns of six cards each, dealing top to bottom so that the left hand column is completed before you lay down the right hand column. Leave slightly more than two card widths between the two columns. Turn the top card of each column 45° outwards from its base. Turn the bottom card in each column 45° outwards from its top.

The spaces between the two columns are reserved for the eight foundation cards, four aces of different suits and four kings of different suits. The aces ascend in sequence to kings, the kings descend in sequence to aces.

If a suitable foundation card – the aces and kings of the four suits – appears in the first twelve cards, put it in position, and put the next card in its place. The entire talon is now dealt out in successive rounds covering the existing cards, top to bottom down the left column, then top to bottom down the right column.

Foundation cards are put in position as soon as they appear in the deal. Cards that marry with those that turn up during the deal can only be played if they are dealt in any of the four corners or on the packet immediately adjoining the foundation to which it belongs.

When a card is withdrawn from the tableau to place on one of the foundations, the next card in the pack is put in its place.

After the deal has been completed these restrictions cease. Marriages, either in descending or ascending order, are made on the twelve packets. And suitable cards can be added to foundation packets, as long as they are the topmost card in a packet.

The sequence of marriages in the outer twelve packets can be reversed. For example, if in one packet there is an ascending married sequence from a three to a nine, and a ten of the same suit is revealed as top card on another packet during the course of play, the nine, eight seven. . . . can be played on top of the ten so that the three becomes the topmost card. This can release cards necessary to build foundation packets.

When all possible moves have been exhausted, the

cards in the outer packets are taken up in order (top corner left on top left, on second top left and so on) redealt and played as before. There are to be only two redeals.

THE FOUR CORNERS

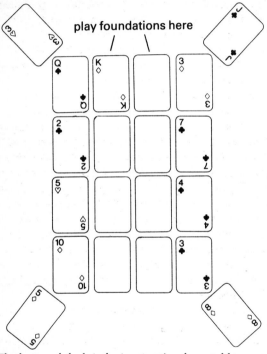

play foundations here

The last card dealt in laying out the above tableau was the king of diamonds, so it was put in position as the first card in its foundation, and the next card in the pack replaced it in the tableau. If, by chance, the second card of the second deal was the queen of diamonds, it could be played immediately onto the king of diamonds next to it. Similarly, if the queen of diamonds was the first, sixth, seventh of twelfth card she could be played on her king as she had would have landed on a corner card.

PERSIAN CARPET

As the tableau is laid into its attractive, intricate pattern you will see how this game gets its name.

You need two packs of cards. Remove an ace and a king of each suit and lay them at the centre of the table as foundation cards. Ace foundations ascend in married sequences to kings: king foundation cards descend in married sequence to aces.

When the foundation cards are in position, deal sixty-four cards in eight rows of eight cards each, laying them vertically and crossways in turn. The first cards in rows 1, 3, 5 and 7 will be vertical and the last cards in these rows will sit crossways. The first cards in rows 2, 4, 6 and 8 will sit crossways and the last cards in these rows will stand vertically.

A card in the layout can be played provided that either of its short sides is not touching another card. So, when the game begins only vertical cards in the top line can be played. When these cards are played, the crossways cards alongside are now available as at least one of their short sides no longer touches another card. The playing of these crossways cards in the top line releases vertical cards in the second line, and play of these cards releases the crossways cards alongside.

Spaces in the layout remain vacant.

The rest of the pack is turned over one by one. Cards that cannot be played on foundation packets are turned face up on the talon. Available cards in the tableau can be removed and played in ascending or descending suit sequences on the talon, thus releasing more cards in the tableau.

The talon is redealt once.

THE SHAH

Take one of the kings of hearts from two packs of cards and place it in the centre of the table. Discard all the other kings: they take no part in the game.

Arrange the eight aces in a circle around the king of hearts. The aces are the foundation cards ascending in suits to the queens, so that if the game comes out the king (the Shah) is surrounded by the eight queens in his harem.

A card is dealt to the outside of each ace: any card that can be played is played immediately; if a two is dealt, it goes on its ace and the vacancy filled by the next card.

Three rounds are played to each point of the star that is forming. Each outside card blocks the ones between it and the aces.

THE SHAH

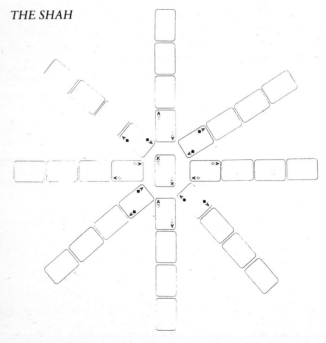

A complete tableau in play.

When the star is complete, examine the cards to decide if any suitable marriages can be made. Marriages can only be made in descending line, remembering that only cards at the end of a ray can be played. Marriages are restricted to cards in the third circle.

When you have played or married all the cards, refill the vacancies from the pack or talon. Vacancies in inner circles are filled first, starting at the top and working clockwise.

The stock is turned over one card at a time: cards that cannot be played on the foundation, married with cards in the star or used to fill vacancies form the talon.

If an entire ray is played, the outer card from one of the seven rays can be moved to fill the vacancy. This often helps the game go on for longer – but seldom helps you get the game out.

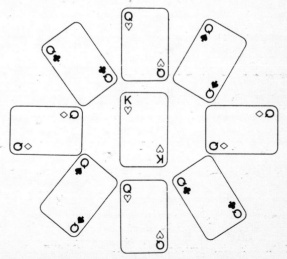

If this Patience works out (but it seldom does) the finished tableau looks like this.

LES QUATORZE

Quatorze is French for fourteen, the all-important number in this game. Deal out twenty-five cards from two packs of cards in five rows of five cards each.

LES QUATORZE

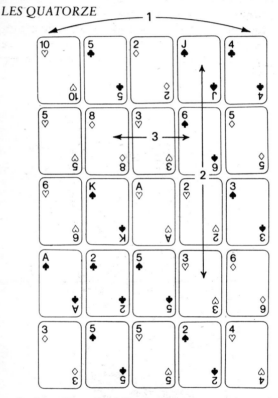

In this tableau the following fourteens can be made:
1. The ten of spades and the four of clubs.
2. The jack of spades and the three of hearts.
3. The eight of diamonds and the six of spades.

Fill the spaces created by pairing cards with cards from hand as soon as a pair has been created.

The object is to compose the number fourteen with any two cards either from a perpendicular or from a horizontal line. Aces are low, knaves count as eleven, queens as twelve and kings as thirteen.

Paired cards are removed from the game. Vacancies are filled with cards from the pack.

The aim of the game is to use all the cards.

If in the course of the game the number fourteen cannot be composed, you have one chance to take any two cards from their proper position to change places with any other two cards.

GAMES FOR TWO

There were two glasses and two chairs,
And two people with one aim:
To cut the pack and deal the cards,
And play to win the game
(*With apologies to Louis MacNeice*)

Some of the best card games are those that have been devised for two players. Some depend on skill: others, like the first one in this section, demand an excellent memory.

PELMANISM

Cut the cards to decide which player is to go first. Now spread the entire pack face down on the table (or floor), making sure that there is a space between each card.

The first player turns over any two cards. If by chance they make a trick, i.e. are the same pip or court value, he removes them from the game and stacks them in front of him. He then turns over another pair of cards and goes on doing so until he turns over two cards that do not form a pair; the cards are turned face down in their original positions. The second player now turns over any two cards . . .

To play Pelmanism players have to remember which cards have been turned over and replaced, so that when they turn over their first card, they know where a suitable partner is located.

The player with most tricks at the end of the game wins.

A more difficult version of the game involves matching colours as well as pips, i.e. the eight of spades with the eight of clubs.

COLONEL

This is a two player version of Rummy: it is played like Rummy with one full pack.

The dealer deals both players ten cards, one at a time. The stock is put on the table between the players and the top card is turned over as the first optional card.

Players aim to build up sequences of three or more cards of the same suit (with aces high) or three or four cards of equal pip or court value.

The non-dealer plays first taking the top card from the stock and assesses its potential for his hand. If he decides to keep it, he discards another card by placing it face up on top of the talon. The upturned talon card now becomes an optional card for the other player, for rather than draw from the stock, players may take the top card from the talon. In either case they have to discard. Players declare sequences and sets by placing them face up in front of them. But players don't have to declare unless they want to: they may want to declare all their cards at once and catch their opponent on the hop at the end of the game. But of course, they run the risk of being caught with all ten cards in hand if their opponent declares first.

Once a sequence or set has been declared, either player can add to it but not until they have declared at least three cards themselves.

When a player has declared all his cards, their total pip value is added to his score: his opponent has the pip value of his declared cards awarded to him, but the pip value of the cards he retains in his hand is added to the winner's score. Court cards and aces score ten points each, others score their pip value.

If the stock is exhausted before either player has declared all his cards, the player with the lower pip value in hand wins that round. He adds the difference between the two scores to his own.

The cards are shuffled between each round.

COLONEL

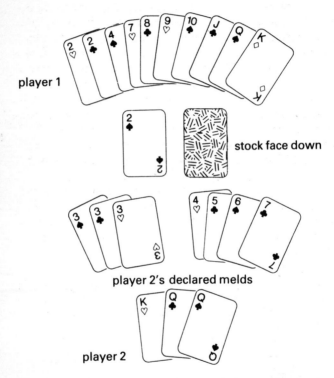

player 1

stock face down

player 2's declared melds

player 2

Player 1 has taken a great risk in not declaring when he could. Player 2 has declared seven cards and has three in hand. But he had discarded a two which is just the card player 1 wants. He takes it from the talon, declares three twos and a sequence of seven, eight, nine, ten, jack, queen and king. He scores 70 points. Player 2 scores 31 for his declarations, but is penalized 30 points for the cards he has in hand.

CRIBBAGE

There can be few pubs that do not have at least one cribbage board somewhere behind the bar. And it is very pleasant indeed to while away an hour supping a pint of good ale over a game of crib with a friend.

The oblong crib or noddy board contains two double lines of thirty holes each, divided for convenience when scoring into groups of five. The board sits between the two players. They both start from the same end, pegging their scores first up the outside row and then down the inside row, once round the board in the 5-card game, twice in the 6-card game and three times in the 7-card game. The first player to return to the hole from which he started wins: so in the 5-card game there are 61 holes, 121 in the 6-card game and 181 in the 7-card one.

Both players use two pegs. If the first score was three, the player would put a peg in the third hole from the beginning: if he next scored ten, he puts his second peg ten holes beyond the first: the hindmost peg is always used to make the score.

The laws are as follows:

1. The cards must be cut at the beginning of each game but not when rubbers are being played. The lowest card cut wins. If there is a tie, a new cut is made.

2. In cutting for deal at least four cards and not more than half the pack should be removed.

3. The cards are dealt one at a time and should not be taken into hand until the deal is complete.

4. If the dealer exposes one of his opponent's cards, the other player is awarded two points and may demand a new card provided he does so before looking at his cards. If a face card is

exposed there must be a new deal.

5. If the dealer misdeals, ie deals too few or too many cards to either player, and the mistake is not seen until the cards are taken to hand, his opponent scores two and there is a redeal.

6. The cards must be shuffled and cut before each redeal.

7. If the non-dealer exposes a card during the deal, the dealer can demand a redeal as long as he does so before he looks at his cards.

8. Both players may shuffle the cards before each deal, but the dealer has the option of the last shuffle.

9. If the non-dealer touches the pack after the cut for start has been made, he forfeits two points.

10. In cutting for start three or four cards must be removed, and not fewer than four cards left on table.

11. When a jack is turned up the dealer is entitled to score 'two for his heels', but he must do so before he plays his first card.

12. There is no penalty if a player neglects to make points.

13. A player who takes more points than he is entitled to when reckoning his hand or crib, or pegging for a penalty or scoring for points made in play, may be put back by as many points as he overscores, and have them added to his opponent's score.

14. A player cannot ask his opponent for help when making out his score.

15. A player has no right to touch his opponent's peg except to put it back when he has overscored. Nor may a player touch his own pegs save for making a score. In either

case, a two-point penalty is incurred. If the front peg has been accidentally displaced it is put back in the hole behind the back peg of the player to whom it belongs. If both pegs are displaced, the opposing player restores them to their places.

16. If either player puts his peg in a hole short of what he has scored, he cannot remove it until he has made another score or points.

17. A player who puts his cards away without scoring for them forfeits any points he might have claimed for them.

18. If a player has scored a game as won, when it is not won, he loses altogether.

19. When a card that may be played legally has been shown, it must by played.

20. In reckoning a hand or crib all the cards of which it consists must be plainly set out and must remain where it is until his opponent has had the opportunity of ascertaining whether the score made on account is accurate.

21. If a player refuses to abide by the rules, his opponent may claim the game.

22. The three points which the non-dealer is permitted to take at the start of each game in 5-card cribbage may be taken during any part of the game.

23. If a player neglects to play when he can without going beyond thirty-one his opponent scores two points.

24. The non-dealer must discard for crib before the dealer. Once a card has been laid out for crib, it cannot be taken up again. Only the dealer may touch the crib but not until he takes it up to count after he has counted his hand. If either player confuses his cards with the crib, he forfeits two points and his

opponent has the option of claiming a new deal.

25. Onlookers are not allowed to interfere with the game.

A full 52-card pack is used. Players cut for dealer with aces low. Aces are also low for scoring sequences when cards rank from ace to king. For counting, kings, queen and ace count ten points each: other cards count their pip value.

Five cards are dealt to each player, the non-dealer pegging three as compensation against the advantage of dealing first in a game. This is known as 'three for last'. After they look at their cards, players put two face down on the dealer's right. These cards are the crib.

The non-dealer now cuts the cards: the dealer turns up the top card of the cut and places it on top of the pack. This is the Start card, and if it is a jack, according to the rules, the dealer pegs his 'two for heels'.

Scores are made both in play which are pegged immediately, and by the scoring values of the cards held in hand which are not pegged until play ends.

During play scores are made by any of the following methods:

1. If a player plays a card of the same rank as the one played immediately before, he pegs two for pair. Court cards can only be paired with cards of equal rank.

2. If a player plays a third card of the same rank as a pair, he scores pair-royal and pegs six.

3. If a player plays a fourth card of the same rank as a pair-royal he pegs twelve for double pair-royal

4. Sequences or runs are pegged one hole for each card, minimum three cards, maximum

seven. Cards need not follow suit and need not be played in sequential order, but a sequence is destroyed by a pair or an intervening card. If, for example, the dealer played a six and the non-dealer a four, the dealer may play a five and peg three. If the non-dealer plays a three or a seven, he pegs four.

5. If a player plays a card which when added to those already played totals fifteen, he pegs two. If the total is thirty-one, he also pegs two. When a player cannot play a card without going over thirty-one he says 'Go!': the other player plays a card or cards bringing the count up to thirty-one limit. If he makes thirty-one exactly he pegs two, otherwise he pegs one for last, thus ending the play.

The non-dealer counts up his score first. The dealer then exposes the crib which is his personal property, pegging any values that he finds in it to his score (and he can make full use of the start card).

If either player holds a jack of the same suit as the start card he pegs 'one for his Nob'. A player holding three cards of the same suit in his hand pegs three for a flush, four if is the same suit as the start card. Nothing is scored for a flush in the crib unless all cards are the same suit as the start card, in which case the dealer pegs five.

Players must count their hands out loud. If a player overlooks any score, his opponent is allowed to call 'Muggins' and peg the score for himself.

If a player reaches his game hole before his opponent has gone half-way round the board, he scores 'lurch' – two games instead of one.

During the game, players add the value of their card to the one played immediately before by the opponent. So, if a six is led, and the other player lays down another six, he pegs two for a pair. If a ten is played and the opponent plays a five he calls 'Fifteen!' and pegs two.

Crib is very hightly rated by card players. The involved calculations it demands and the endless variety of chances that can be created makes it an amusing and fascinating game.

There are versions of cribbage for three or four players, but the two-man game is the most satisfactory.

CASINO

The simplicity of play in Casino belies the skill necessary to win: for an excellent memory and the ability to deduce what cards one's opponent is holding are essential to play the game well.

Cut for dealer. The winner deals two cards face downwards to his opponent, two face upwards onto the table, two face downwards to himself: he then does the same again, so that at the end of the deal both players have four hidden cards and there are four open cards in the tableau. (The same dealer deals in all future rounds of the rubber).

The stock of forty cards is placed face downwards on the table.

Aces count as one, non-court cards at their pip value and court cards, which are only used for pairing, have no pip value.

Scoring is as follows:

Twenty-seven or more cards (Majority): 3 points.

The ten of diamonds (Great Casino): 2 points.

The two of spades (Little Casino): 1 point.

Seven or more spades (Majority in spades): 1 point.

Aces: 1 point each.

The Sweep (all cards in the tableau): 1 point.

Players have the following options:

Pairing: playing a card of equal value to one in the

tableau. If a player has a six in his hand, he plays it and take all the sixes in the tableau as a trick. Court cards can only be paired one at a time.

The layout

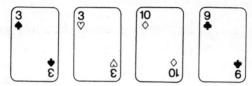

Pairing *The player with this hand can play his three from hand and take the two threes from the layout.*

Combining: playing one card from the hand and taking cards whose pip value adds up to it from the tableau. For example, if a player leads a seven, he could take a four and a three, five and a two, or six and ace from the tableau.

Combining *The player with these cards can combine by playing the six of spades and taking the two threes from the layout above.*

Building: creating future tricks playing a card from the hand onto a card on the tableau, so that they combine to total the pip value of another card in the player's hand. For example if a player has a three and a four in his hand and there is an ace in the layout, he may lay the three from his hand onto the ace, so that next time it is his turn he plays the four and takes the three cards (four, three and ace) as a trick. The danger in building is that the opponent may be able to take the trick first if he has a suitable card in his hand. Either player can add to a build, up to a maximum of five cards. A built packet cannot be used to combine: it must be taken as one unit.

Building *This player can play the two of clubs onto a three in the layout (see top, page 43) and (as long as his opponent does not forestall him) on his next turn can play the five of diamonds taking the three and the two for a trick.*

Calling: is an extension of building whereby players can put their marker on one or more combinations for later capture. If a player has two cards of equal pip value in his hand, and there is a suitable combination on the table, he could play one of them and take the combination cards as a trick or he can can call, by playing one of the two cards from his hand onto one of the non-combination cards.

For example if the player holds two nines in his hand and there is a six and a three on the table he could play one nine, combine it with the six and three and take a three card trick. Better to cover one of the other two cards on table with one of the nines, so that next time he plays he lays down the nine from his hand, takes the nine played last time and the combination nine (the six and the three), thus giving him a four-card trick.

Calling *This player puts one of his nines on either the eight or the jack in the layout. Next time he plays (again as long as his opponent has not forestalled him) his second nine, and takes the nine, six and the three from the layout.*

Trailing: occurs when none of the above moves can be made. A card must be played from hand to the layout. It is best to play a low card but not an ace, two of spades, Little Casino, or another spade. If there are no cards in the layout, the only possible play is to trail.

The first round continues until both players have played the four cards in their hand by pairing, combining, building, calling or trailing.

The dealer now deals four cards each, but none to the layout, and the second round begins.

Play continues until the stock is finished: so there are six deals in a rubber. Before dealing the last cards, the dealer must declare it as the last round. If he forgets, his opponent has the right to cancel the entire rubber.

The winner of the last trick in the final deal takes all the cards left in the layout, and the rubber is scored. The player with the most points wins.

If a player starts a build without the card in hand to take the trick in a later round, he forfeits the game. The same penalty is incurred if a player trails when he can make another play.

If the dealer exposes a card during the deal, other than to the table, that card goes to the layout and the dealer plays the hand with three cards.

There are a few variations. In Royal Casino. aces count as one or fourteen, kings as thirteen, queens as twelve and jacks as eleven, and can be used for combining and building: a queen and a two could take an ace, an eight and a three take a jack, and so on.

There is only one deal in Stock Casino, the stock being placed face downward on the table and drawn from after each move to bring the number of cards in players' hands to four.

Casino can of course be played for money. It is best to keep the stakes small as substantial scores can be buit up. A player agreeing to an innocent 'penny–a–point OK?' may have to pay out more than he bargains for.

CALIFORNIA JACK

Cut the cards for dealer. The loser then cuts the cards for trumps, before the dealer deals six cards to both players and places the stock face up in the middle of the table, making sure that the cards are squared up so that only the top card can be seen.

The non-dealer leads for the first trick. Players must follow suit (a revoke costs one point). If they can't, they discard or trump.

Whoever wins the trick takes the top card from the stock: the loser takes the one beneath.

When there are no more cards in the stock and the last six tricks have been won or lost, players count up, scoring for High, Low, Jack and Game.

The game is won by the player with the highest score: one point is scored for winning High (winning a trick with the ace of trumps), one point for winning Low (winning a trick with the two of trumps), one point for Jack (winning a trick with the jack of trumps) and one point for Game, having the majority of points in the tricks each player has taken counting four points for each ace won, three for each king won, two for each queen won and one for each jack won, with a bonus of ten for each ten won.

When playing California Jack, it is best to try to keep both winning and losing cards in hand, for, if the top card in the stock is a useless one, you will want to lose the trick so that your opponent is forced to take it.

A version of the game can be played in which the stock is placed face down. It is called SHASTA SAM but requires less skill as the card being played for is unseen, and so players do not know whether or not to go for it.

PINOCLE

Two packs of cards are required to play this game. Remove all cards below nine so that you have a 48-card pack containing the two aces, kings, queens, jacks, tens and nines of each suit.

Both players are dealt twelve cards, three or four at a time rather than the more normal one at a time.

The twenty-fifth card is exposed on the table to indicate the trump suit. The rest of the pack is placed face downwards on the table covering the trump indicator.

Players aim to take tricks that contain cards which score points when they are won in a trick. They also score by melding certain combinations of cards.

The following cards score when taken in a trick:

Aces: 11 points each.

Tens: 10 points each.

Kings: 4 points each.

Queens: 3 points each.

Jacks: 2 points each.

Whoever takes the last trick is awarded a 10-point bonus.

Melds are classified in the following categories:

Class A Melds

Ace, ten, King, Queen and Jack of the trump suit: 150 points.

King and Queen of trump suit (a royal marriage): 40 points.

King and Queen of a plain suit (a common marriage): 20 points.

Class B Melds

Spade Queen and Diamond Jack – Pinocle: 40 points.

Nine of trumps – Dis: 10 points.

Class C Melds

Four aces one of each suit: 100 points.

Four kings one of each suit: 80 points.

Four queens one of each suit: 60 points.

Four jacks one of each suit: 40 points.

The non-dealer leads the first card. Thereafter the winner of a trick leads to the next. Players do not have to follow suit. The player who takes the trick takes the top card off the stock. The loser takes the next one.

Between winning a trick and drawing from the stock, a player can meld any of the above according to these rules:

1. A player may only meld once per turn.
2. At least one card must come from hand and be placed on the table for each meld.
3. If a card has been melded, it can be melded again as long as it is used in a different class or in a higher-scoring meld in the same class; e.g. if hearts are trumps, a player can meld royal marriage and as melds are scored as soon as they are declared, he scores forty points. He can then add ace, ten and jack on a later declaration and score 150 points. But, he cannot declare sequence and later, remove the king and queen to declare royal marriage.

A player melds by placing the cards face upwards on the table in front of him: the cards stay there until either he decides to use them to take a trick or until the stock is exhausted.

If the dis turns up as the trump card, the dealer scores ten points. A player holding the dis may count it simply by showing it when winning a trick. He may count the dis and make a meld at the same time. After winning a trick, the player who holds the dis is allowed to exchange it for a trump card.

The player who takes the twelfth trick can meld if he is able. He then draws the last unexposed card from the stock and shows it to the other player who takes the exposed last card.

They now play the last twelve tricks when the rules change.

A player must follow suit: if he can't, he must trump if he can. If a trump card is led, the other player must take the trick if he can.

The players add their score for cards taken in tricks after the hand is played. Scores of seven, eight or nine are counted as ten.

Skilled Pinocle players have good memories: when playing the last twelve tricks, a good player will know his opponent's hand to the last card. He will also be able to assess the advantage of winning the last trick played before the stock is exhausted. He will know whether to win it and make a meld if he can, thus stopping his opponent scoring for a final meld, or lose it which gives his opponent the chance to meld but gives him another trump card for the play off.

CHINESE PATIENCE

Whoever wins the cut, deals the pack one card at a time, starting with his opponent. Four times in the deal, the non-dealer says 'Now' and the next card is placed face up in the centre of the table.

Players do not look at their hands: they place them face down in a neat packet in front of them.

The aim is to have all fifty-two cards in your opponent's packet.

The non-dealer picks up the top card from his packet. If he can he plays it on one of the cards in the tableau, alternate colours ascending or descending in sequence – black eight on red seven or red nine, and so on. If he plays, he turns over the next card in his packet, continuing to play and turn over until he gets an unplayable card. This goes face up alongside his packet to start his talon.

The dealer now turns up the top card in his packet. He can play it on the tableau or on his opponent's talon. He can now, if there are suitable cards, play them from the tableau onto his opponent's talon, again in alternate colours in ascending or

descending sequences. Aces are high or low. Therefore if there's an ace on talon or tableau, either a
king can be played to start a descending sequence, or
a two to start an ascending one. Reversed sequences
are allowed on the talon or tableau: e.g. if a black
six had been placed on a red five, the next card to be
played on it can be either a red seven or the other
red five.

When a packet in the tableau is vacant, whoever's
turn it is fills it with his next card.

When there are no cards left in either player's
tableau, the top card in the talon is used as the
starter card in the next one, and the rest of the talon
are turned as the new packet.

CHINESE PATIENCE

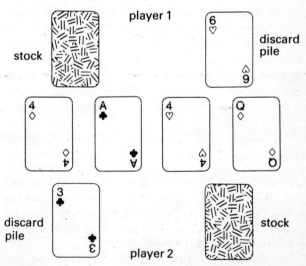

*If the next card turned over by player 2 is a five, he can
play it on his opponent's discard pile, then put either
four on the five, the three from his own discard pile on
the four and the other four onto the three.*

COMET

You need two 52-card packs with the same design on the backs. Remove all the aces. Divide the remaining cards into two packs, one containing all the red cards and the other all the black cards. Put a red nine in the black pack and a black nine in the red pack.

Use the black pack for the first round, the red for the second and so on, using the packs alternately thereafter.

Each player is dealt eighteen cards. Put the remaining twelve cards on one side. They are not needed until the third round when they are shuffled in with the rest of the pack.

The non-dealer leads by playing any card he wants to face upwards in the centre of the table. The players now take it in turn to build on it by rank.

If a six is led, the second player can put as many

COMET

player 1

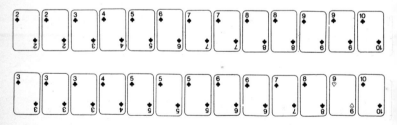

player 2

sevens as he has in his hand on it. The sequence continues until either player is unable to build on it – a stop. Whoever played the stop card (the king is always a stop) leads any card from his hand to begin the next sequence.

The odd-coloured nine is the Comet, representing any card its holder wishes and must be played in turn. It is a stop: whoever plays it, starts the next sequence.

The first player to get rid of all his cards is the winner, scoring the total pip value of the remaining cards in his opponent's hand with court cards counting ten each. If a player is left holding the Comet, the winner is awarded double the pip value of the cards in the loser's hand. If the winner gets out by playing the Comet nominated as another card, he doubles his score: if he wins by playing it as a nine, his score is quadrupled.

Player 1 to lead any card he wants. If he led the three of clubs, play could go:

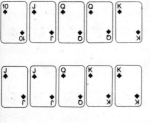

Player 1	Player 2
3C	4S
5S	6S and 6C
7S and 7C	8C
9S and 9C	10S
JC	QC
KS stop	–
4C	5C, 5C and 5S
6S	7S
8C and 8S	9H (Comet) stop
–	KC stop
–	KC stop
–	JC
QC and QS stop	–
10C and 10S	JS stop
–	3S, 3S and 3C stop and win

GERMAN WHIST

Cut a 52-card pack to decide which of the two players is going to deal: Aces are high. Whoever wins deals thirteen cards to himself and his opponent, puts the remaining twenty-six cards face down in the centre of the table, and turns over the top one to decide the trump suit for the first round.

The dealer's opponent is first to go, playing any card he wants to from his hand. His opponent must follow suit. If he can't, he discards or plays a trump card. Whichever player takes the trick puts it face down in front of him and then takes the top, exposed, card from the stock. The loser takes the next one, but doesn't show it to his opponent. The suit of the next card in the stock is trumps for the

GERMAN WHIST

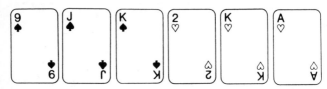

dealer's hand

second hand

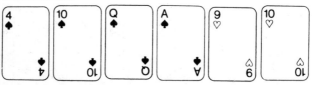

Sort cards into suits. The non-dealer leads first.

second round. The winner of the first trick leads in the second round.

After thirteen tricks have been played, both players have twelve cards in their hand and there are two cards in the stock, the upturned top one having been trump for the previous round. The player who won the thirteenth trick takes that card: whichever suit it is remains trump for the rest of the game. His opponent takes the last unseen card.

The game continues until all the cards have been played. Whoever takes most tricks is the winner, and scores two points. If both players take thirteen tricks, they score one point each.

Set a limit on the game – first to reach an agreed number of points wins the match.

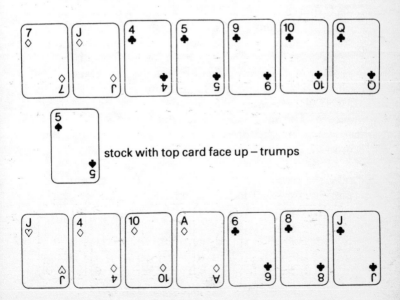

stock with top card face up – trumps

GAMES FOR THREE

Three is the minimum number of players for these games. Some of them can be played by more.

FIVE HUNDRED

Remove all twos, threes, fours, fives and sixes from a 52-card pack, shuffle a joker into the remaining cards and deal in bundles of three-two-three-two so that everyone has ten cards: the remaining three cards – the widow – are placed face down on the table. Whoever wins the bidding takes the widow and discards any three cards from his hand, unseen by the other players.

The player on the dealer's left starts the bidding, declaring that he will take a specified number of tricks in the suit of his choice. The minimum bid is six tricks in any suit. The lowest ranked suit is spades, ascending through clubs, diamonds and hearts to no-trump. A bid in a higher value suit outranks a bid for the same number of tricks in a lower value suit. Each bid must outrank the one before. The final bid decides the trump suit.

A player who passes cannot enter or re-enter the bidding at a later stage.

If all three players pass, no one has the right to take the widow, the hand is played in no trump and players are awarded a straight ten points for each trick taken.

The trump cards rank as follows: joker, jack of trumps (which is called the right bower), jack of the suit of the same colour (the left bower), ace, king, queen, ten, nine, eight and seven.

Cards in non-trump suits descend in rank from ace to seven.

There are therefore ten cards in the trump suit, seven in the non-trump suit of the same colour, and eight in the other two suits.

When a round is being played in no trump, there are eight cards in each suit, as there are no bower cards. But in practice there may be nine cards in one suit in a no trump round because if the joker is led, whoever leads it nominates its suit and it must win the trick as it will outrank other cards in that suit. Whoever leads the joker cannot nominate it to be a suit he has previously renounced (discarded on). If a player plays the joker on another card it will win unless he has previously renounced in that suit.

The first player to reach a score of 500 wins the game. Scoring is as follows:

Tricks bid

	6	7	8	9	10
No trump	120	220	320	420	520
Hearts	100	200	300	400	500
Diamonds	80	180	280	380	480
Clubs	60	160	260	360	460
Spades	40	140	240	340	440

Players score the value of their contract if they make it. There is no bonus for overtricks, but if a bidder takes all ten tricks (the slam) whether or not he bid it, he is awarded a bonus of 250 if his contract was for less than that: if the contract was for more than 250 points, he is awarded a bonus equal to the contract score for making the slam.

It is possible for a player to take game in one deal. If, for example, a player bid eight clubs and takes all ten tricks, he would score 260 for making his contract plus a bonus of 260, making a total of 520 points.

The player who makes the contract leads: the others must follow suit: if they can't they may trump or discard. As the joker and left bower both count as trump cards, other players must play trumps if either are led: only the right bower or joker can beat the left bower.

If a player fails to make a contract, the two who defeated him *both* score the value of the contract, otherwise they score ten points for each trick they take.

If two players reach game in the same round, the one who is declarer wins the game as long as he makes his contract. If neither of the players who break 500 is the declarer, the one who first takes sufficient tricks to reach 500 wins.

KNAVES

Players are dealt seventeen cards each. The remaining card decides trump for that round. Play follows normal convention: the player on the dealer's left leads: highest card played wins: players must follow suit if they can, otherwise they trump or discard.

Players score one point for each trick taken and the first player to reach twenty points wins.

BUT, players are penalized for any trick taken containing a jack: they lose four points for taking the jack of hearts, three for the jack of diamonds, two for the jack of clubs, and one for the jack of spades.

So a player who builds up a substantial ·lead usually finds that the other two combine to force him to take tricks for which he will be penalized.

Players who hold jacks should not lead them. This gives other players the opportunity to play lower, forcing whoever leads the card to take the trick. Similarly, players should avoid leading aces, kings and queens of a suit in which the jack has not yet been played, as whoever holds it will be able to get rid of it.

OKLAHOMA

Oklahoma is played like Rummy but players can only add to their own sequences. Shuffle two 52-card packs and one joker and deal thirteen cards to each player. The stock is placed face down in the centre of the table. The top card is turned over and placed beside the stock as the first card in the talon. The player on the dealer's left has the right to take the exposed card. If he doesn't want it the player on his left can take it and so on round the table. A player who takes the card must meld it immediately with at least two cards in his hand, declare them and replace the talon card with an unwanted card from his hand.

If no player takes the exposed card, the player on the dealer's left draws the top card. He either keeps it, in which case he discards another, turning it face up beside the stock as the first card in the talon, or, he discards it straight away if it is no use to him. Players can only declare after they have drawn from the stock, but before they discard onto the talon.

When play is under way, a player who takes the exposed card from the talon must meld it and declare immediately. Declarations may be a minimum of three cards in suit sequences with aces high or low: the maximum meld is fourteen cards in running suits, ace to ace. No more than four cards of the same pip value may be melded as a set.

If a player takes the exposed card on top of the discard pile he must immediately meld it and then take the other cards in the discard pile, make any more melds, and then discard.

The joker and all twos are wild cards, used to represent any card elected by the player who announces what it is as soon as he makes a declaration. A player who draws a card represented by a wild card in one of his melds, may remove the wild card from the meld, replace it with the card it stood for, and use the wild card in a new meld. He cannot exchange the wild cards if they sit in the melds of another player.

The game finishes when a player has melded all his cards. But he must, of course, discard after he plays out. If he holds say two fives and draws a third, he cannot declare them as he would have nothing to discard. Players who are left with two cards, can only hope to get out by drawing cards that can be added to existing runs and sequences. If, for example, a player has declared a run of ace, two and three of clubs and holds the five plus another card, he could get out if he drew the four by adding the four and five to his sequence and discarding his useless card.

If a player holds the queen of spades, he can use it in a meld, but it can only be discarded by the player holding it when he has no other card to get rid of.

Players are awarded the pip value of all the cards they have declared and are penalized for the cards still held, the total being added to the winner's score.

The first player out is awarded a bonus of 100.

Scoring is as follows:

	If played	If in hand
Joker	+100	−200
Queen of spades	+ 50	−100
Ace	+ 20	− 20
A two representing cards from king to 8 (excluding the queen of spades)	+ 10	− 20
Cards from king to 8 (including the queen of spades)	+ 10	− 10
7, 6, 5, 4, 3	+ 5	− 5
2 representing cards from 7 down	nil	− 20

The winner is the first player to reach 1,000 points.

If a player draws the last card from the stock and discards without going out, the scores are totalled but no one receives the 100 winning bonus. Neither does a player who goes out on his first turn.

A player who goes out on or after his second turn and who has not previously made a meld, is said to go out concealed and receives 250 points.

The first player to reach 1000 receives a bonus of 200 points, if two or more players reach 1000 in the same deal, the player with the higher score wins: the 200 bonus is divided between them.

RUMMY

The aim of Rummy is to get rid of all the cards in your hand and to score as many points as you can.

Cut the pack for dealer and deal the cards to each player. If there are three or four players, deal seven cards each: if there are five or six players, deal six cards each.

After the cards have been dealt put the stock face down on the table, turn over the top card and lay it next to the stock. This card is the first of the waste pile.

Players can lay down sequences of cards such as three or four of a kind (three sevens for example) or consecutive runs of the same suit, with a minimum of three cards in the run (the seven, eight and nine of diamonds for example).

Aces are low in Rummy, so a sequence of four aces scores four points. The highest possible four-card run is ten, knave, queen and king of a suit. This would score forty points – ten, the pip value of the ten, and ten for each of the court cards. Other cards score their pip value.

Players take it in turn to draw a card from the stock. If they want to keep it they put it in their hands and put an unwanted card, face up on top of the waste pile. If the card is no use to them, they put it face up on top of the waste pile. When it is his turn a player can either take the top card from the stock or from the waste pile. When there are no cards left in the stock, the waste pile is turned face down on the table to become the new stock, with the last top card, face up, the first card in the new waste pile.

Players have to wait their turn before declaring (laying down cards). But even if they have a run or a sequence, they don't have to declare it until they want to.

A player who lays down all his cards in one move has 'gone Rummy'.

As well as creating their own runs and sequences, players can add to those of other players. So if someone has three tens displayed, another player can declare a fourth ten by laying it alongside his own declarations. But cards can only be played like this by players who have already declared a run or prial (three cards of equal pip value) of their own.

When a player has declared all his cards, the round is over. Players add the pip value of all the cards they have declared to their own score. Cards that they still have in their hands are deducted from their score. If a player has won by going rummy, double the pip value of the cards the other players have in their hand is added to the winner's score.

Rummy players try to confuse each other into believing that they are collecting a certain pip value card or suit when, in fact, they are looking for something else. By doing this they hope that players will discard cards useful to them. Players, of course, try not to discard cards that they think will be useful to the player on their left.

Players have to decide whether to lay cards down

as soon as they can: this increases their own scores, but gives other players the chance to get rid of unwanted cards by adding to declared prials and melds. But a player waiting to try to 'go Rummy' runs the risk of being caught with a massive seven-card score which is added to the winner's total.

RUMMY

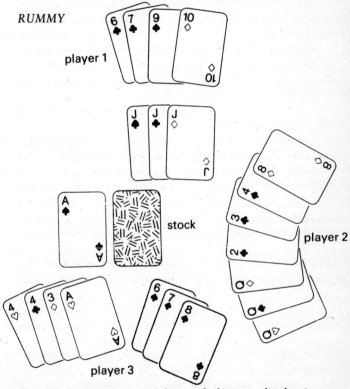

Player 2 has taken a risk by not declaring earlier but it has paid off. He takes the card that has just been discarded, declares three queens, a sequence of ace, two, three, four and discards the eight of diamonds. Player 1 scores −2 (30–32): player 2 scores 40: and player 3 scores 9 (21–12).

KNOCK-OUT WHIST

Three is the minimum number of players for Knock-Out Whist. Cut for dealer and give everyone seven cards each. The player on the dealer's left cuts to decide the trump suit for the first round and plays the first card. Players have to follow suit: whoever plays the highest card (with aces high) in the round wins the trick and leads.

Players who are unable to follow suit can play a trump card (if they have any) which assumes a higher value than the ace of the suit led and so wins the trick. If a card is trumped, it can be over-trumped by another player who lacks cards in the suit led by playing a higher value trump card.

The player who takes most tricks in the first round calls trumps for the second round. If two players have taken the same number of tricks, they cut to decide who gets the advantage of calling trumps. The second round of six cards each is dealt by the player on the left hand side of the original dealer. Whoever calls trumps leads. The third round is five cards each, the fourth four cards each and so on.

In the first three rounds, a player who fails to take any tricks is given a single card – 'a dog's chance'. He can ask for it whenever he wants during the deal and play it whenever he wants during that round. If he succeeds in taking a trick with his single card he is dealt a full hand in the following round. If his card is a loser, he is out of the game, for a player can only claim one 'dog's chance' a game.

The game can be won outright in the fourth, fifth and sixth rounds if one player takes all the tricks. If it goes on to the seventh round, the two surviving players cut for trump and are dealt one card each; in a case like this it doesn't matter who plays the first card!

KNOCK-OUT WHIST

player 1

It's the third round and player 1 is to call trumps.
'Spades!'

Trick	Player 1	Player 2	Player 3
1	leads 6C	7C	2C
2	9H	leads AH	3H
3	7S	leads QH	3D
4	leads 10S	5S	4D
5	leads 10D	KH	5D

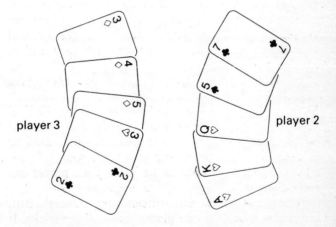

player 3   player 2

Player 3 takes no tricks: he's out. Player 2 takes 2
tricks. Player 1 takes 3 tricks, and calls trumps for the
next round when four cards are dealt to both remaining
players.

OLD MAID

Take the queen of hearts from a pack and deal face down to each player. Players sort their hands into pairs – two kings, two nines or whatever – and discard each pair onto a central pile so that they are left with hands in which no two cards are the same.

The dealer offers his hand to the player on his left making sure that he can't see the cards. This player takes one card from it and if he can make a pair with the card he's taken, adds them to the central pile. If he is unable to make a pair, he keeps the card in his hand. He in turn offers his cards to the player on his left. Players who get rid of all their cards stay in the game, selecting a card from the player on their right, and offering it to the player on their left.

As there are three queens, one of them is certain to be the last card in the game, and whoever is left with it loses the game and drops out for the next round.

A similar game is played in France whereby all the jacks except the jack of spades are removed from the pack before it is dealt. The jack of spades is called *le vieux garçon* which is the name of the game. Whoever is left with the single jack is the loser.

CHEAT

You can play Cheat with more than three players but three is best. If you are going to play with four or more players, use two packs.

Cut for dealer who deals *all* the cards . . . as the aim of the game is to get rid of all your cards and as anything goes, make sure that the dealer deals himself the same number of cards as everyone else.

The player on the dealer's left starts the game by putting face down whatever card or cards he wants. If he put down three nines he would call 'Three nines!' But there's no guarantee that he has, in fact, played what has been claimed: a skilful player may have put down five cards and none of them need be nines. (If you intend to cheat by putting down more cards than you call, it's best to wait until several players have gone, so that there are already cards in the central packet before you play.)

Players can play cards of the same value as those just played or one pip up, so the next player can continue either with nines or tens.

Players can call 'Cheat!' at any time. Whoever has just gone has then to turn over the cards he put on the stock. If the charge is proven, he takes *all* the cards in the stock. If he proves that he played exactly what he called out, then his accuser takes the stock.

Players try to convince others that they are cheating when they are innocent: and that they are honest when they are in fact lying.

It's best that players don't call 'Cheat!' unless they are fairly certain that the charge will stand. Obviously if someone calls 'Three sevens' say, and another player holds two sevens in his hand, he would be silly to stay silent.

Of course, whoever plays his last card or cards first and claims the game must be accused of cheating, for there is nothing to lose at that stage. If he was honest and laid what he called, he wins the game anyway: but if he has been cheating, he's back in the game again.

GAMES FOR FOUR

BLACK LADY

Seven is the maximum number for a game of Black Lady, also known as Black Maria or Calamity Jane.

To ensure that each player receives the same number of cards, remove deuces from a 52-card pack as follows:

Players	Cards dealt to each player	Deuces removed from pack
4	13	–
5	10	2
6	8	4
7	7	3

After the deal, players select three cards from their hands, and put them on the table between themselves and the player on their left. When everyone has laid down their three cards, they take the three cards that the player on their right has discarded.

The game is played in no trump. The player on the dealer's left leads. The others follow suit, the trick being taken by the highest card played in the suit led. Players who cannot follow suit discard.

The object of the game is to avoid taking the queen of spades (the eponymous Black Lady) and any penalty cards. OR to take *all* the hearts *and* the queen of spades.

If a player takes the Black Lady and *all* the hearts, nobody scores. Otherwise players are charged one point for each heart they take and thirteen points for taking the Black Lady. The ace of spades counts seven penalty points, the king ten. Players drop out of the game as soon as they reach 100 points. The winner is the last player left in.

WHIST

When Whist first developed from the game Triumph, it was immensely popular with working class folk. But in the early eighteenth century it was taken up by Lord Folkstone and his fashionable set who frequented the Crown Coffee House in London. They knew the game as Whisk. After Edmond Hoyle published his first treatise on the game in 1742 it spread like wildfire among 'the upper ten thousand' – the cream of London society. Players became so engrossed in the game that anyone making an unnecessary noise was instantly told to 'whist', hence Whist. Some people ranked it the most important of their pastimes, well almost the most important as Charles Lamb noted in his essay *Mrs Battle's Opinions of Whist*.

' "A clear fire, a clean hearth and the rigour of the game." This was the celebrated wish of old Sarah Battle (now with God) who, next to her devotions, loved a good game of whist.'

Whist is essentially a very simple game. Two players, sitting facing each other across the table, play against the other pair.

The usual way of deciding dealer for the first game is for all four players to draw from the pack, spread face down on the table. Whoever draws the highest card, with aces by convention the lowest card, deals. Cards are shuffled between each deal.

Each player is dealt thirteen cards, starting with the player on the dealer's left. The last card is laid face up for all to see. It decides trump for the game: the dealer then adds it to his hand.

The player on the dealer's left leads. The others must follow suit. Only if they are unable to do so may they trump or discard. The trick is won by whoever plays the highest card of the suit led, or the highest trump. Revoking incurs a penalty of three points. The player who wins a trick, leads for the following one.

Game is won when one side has scored five points: a rubber is best of three games. Pairs have to take at least seven tricks to score. The first six tricks taken are known as the book and score nothing. Thereafter each trick taken counts as one point.

Points are also given for honour cards held. If a side is dealt ace, king, queen and jack of the trump suit they score four points. A side dealt three honours scores two points. If, however, at the beginning of a deal a side already has four points, it cannot claim an honours score.

Successful whist playing demands close collaboration between partners. Because there are certain conventions demanding that card play depends on other cards held in hand, after a trick or two, good players should be able to build up an accurate picture of the cards held by partner and opposition and play accordingly.

The first chance players have of giving partner a clue to what they have in their hands is when they lead. The general rule is to lead the fourth card from the longest suit held, unless you have any of the following combinations:

| | Trump Suit | |
Cards held	First lead	Second lead
Four honours	J	Q
Three top honours	Q	K
Seven or more cards to ace, king	K	A
Six cards to ace, king	4th best	

Plain suits

Cards held	First lead	Second lead
Four honours	K	J
Three top honours	K	Q
Three or more cards to ace, king	K	A
Ace, king	A	K
King, queen, jack and one more	Q	J
King, queen, jack and two more	J	K
Six or more cards to king, queen, jack	J	Q
Six or more cards to ace	A	4th next best
Four or more to king, queen	K	" " "
Ace, queen, jack	A	Q
Ace, queen, jack and one more	A	Q
Five or more to ace, queen, jack	A	J
King, jack, ten and nine	9	K (if the ace or queen is played)
Three cards to queen, jack	Q	–
Five or more cards to queen jack	4th best	–

The following sample hand demonstrates the leads and play. As a general rule, if a hand contains none of the above combinations, lead the fourth card from the strongest suit. Another general rule to remember is that the player who is second to the trick should play low.

```
                        North
                        S 8, 4
                        H A, 7, 5, 3
                        D J, 8, 5, 2
                        C Q, 7, 2
        West                                East
S 9, 6, 5                                    S K, 7, 3
H K, 10, 8, 4, 2                             H J, 9
D A, K                                       D Q, 10, 7, 6, 4
C K, 10, 6                                   C J, 5, 4
                        South
                        S A, Q, J, 10, 2
                        H Q, 6
                        D 9, 3
                        C A, 9, 8, 3
```

East deals. Clubs are turned up trump. South leads.

Trick 1: South's strongest suit is spades. He leads the ace signalling to his partner that he has five or more with top honours apart from the king. West, North and East follow suit with their lowest spades.

Trick 2: South leads the spade jack hoping to draw the king, so leaving his queen high. West plays the six, North the eight (leaving him void in the suit) and East takes the trick with the king.

Trick 3: East leads the fourth best (the six) of his strongest suit (diamonds). South, second to play, plays low. West's king takes the trick. North follows suit with his lowest diamond.

Trick 4: West could signal to his partner that

hearts is his strongest suit by playing the H4. But as the suit is not particularly strong and there has been only one round of diamonds, he leads the ace, hoping for even diamond distribution. It holds. North plays D5, East D4 and South D9. As East led a diamond and North had four in his hand, North can be fairly certain that either his partner or West is void in the suit. As it happens both are, but North should be aware that as West did not return a low diamond to his partner, but played the ace, West is void.

Trick 5: West now leads the fourth card of his strongest suit, H4. North plays low. East plays HJ and South takes the trick with HQ.

Trick 6: South now has control in spades, a singleton heart, is void in diamonds and four trumps to the ace. If he can establish his three spade tricks, with the ace of trumps, he has four tricks in hand. If North has one trick in hand, that will give them seven tricks and a point towards game. Neither West nor East led clubs when they had the chance to do so, suggesting that they have little trump strength. So South leads a low club, the three. West, second in hand plays low, the six. He could, as the cards sit, have taken the trick with the king, but if North had had the ace, West would lose his king to it. Best to play low. North take the trick with the queen. East plays the four.

Trick 7: North returns a low club. East thinks to himself 'Everyone knows I have the jack of trumps, it was revealed as the card that decided the trump suit. If South had held ace, king and two more, it would more than likely have been his strongest suit and he would have led it first time round. I'm second to play, so I should play low anyway. If South has the king and partner the ace, the king will fall to the ace, leaving my jack a winner: if South has ace, and partner the king and one more, South will take the trick, giving us two trump tricks, as long as a trump is not led later.' So, East plays his C5, South comes up with ace and West the C10.

Trick 8: South now thinks 'There are five trumps left. I have two of them. I know East has the jack. That leaves two. If either West or East had had the two, they would have played it on trick six, so North must have it. If he had the king as well he would have led it at the last trick, as he should have known that I had the ace. So if I lead a club, the king and the jack will fall to it.' He leads his C8, and the outstanding trumps are played.

North and South are now sure of at least four of the last five tricks. If West leads his last spade, South takes his three spade tricks, leads his remaining trump at trick twelve. North is sure to hold on to his heart ace which takes the last trick on South's lead of H6. With ten tricks taken, North/South score four points.

If West leads a low heart, North takes it with his ace (at this stage in the game second to trick doesn't play low – he takes any tricks he can). He should have worked out that South has the last trump, and that he is probably void in diamonds. So he leads D8, trumped by South who takes his three spade tricks, and concedes that last trick to West's king.

With nine tricks, North/South score three points towards game.

Even if North is a complete novice and doesn't take a heart lead with his ace, South is certain of the last four of the last five tricks. A heart lead from West, leaves him void in both diamonds and hearts, and with control in spades and the outstanding trump, nothing can stop him.

A good grounding in Whist is excellent training for what most players consider to be the king of card games – Bridge.

Sadly, it is not possible to deal with the intricacies of bidding and playing involved in Bridge in this book. Countless books have been written on the game.

SOLO WHIST

Solo whist probably originated in Belgium where it is still widely played with great enthusiasm.

Players are dealt thirteen cards each after the cards have been shuffled. Any player may shuffle, but the dealer has the right to shuffle last.

The cards are dealt in batches of three at a time, followed by a single card. The last card is turned up on the table as the preferred trump.

Players assess their hands to determine how many tricks they can take. Bids are as follows:

Value	*Bid*	*Meaning*
2	Proposal and acceptance	Two players will form a partnership, contracting to take eight tricks in the preferred trump.
2	Solo	The caller will take five tricks in the preferred trump, playing against all the other players.
3	Misere	The caller wants to play the hand on his own in no trump, aiming to take no tricks.
4	Abundance	The caller will decide the trump suit and take nine tricks.

Value	Bid	Meaning
4	Royal abundance	The caller accepts the preferred trump and contracts to make nine tricks.
6	Spread misere	The caller wants the hand played in no trump. He will lay his cards face up on the table and he will take no tricks.
8	Declared abundance	Caller will take thirteen tricks played in no trumps (some solo players allow a bid of declared abundance to be played in a trump suit of the caller's choosing).

If a caller makes the tricks he called, or more, the other players pay him the value of his call. If he fails to make the bid, he pays its value to each of the other players.

The player on the dealer's left is said to hold the 'eldest hand' and is first to bid. Players can pass or bid. Bids must be higher than the one before. Once a player passes, he may not re-enter the bidding unless he holds the eldest hand in which case he can accept a proposal. If a player bids proposal, and no one accepts it he can either pass or up his bid to solo.

Play begins when a bid has been established by being followed by three passes. The dealer takes the preferred trump card into hand. If the hand is being played in abundance, the caller announces the trump suit. The eldest hand leads to the first trick except in a hand of declared abundance, in which case the caller leads to the first trick. Thereafter, whoever takes a trick leads to the next one. The usual rules apply: players play to the trick clockwise in turn, and can only trump if they cannot follow suit.

If all players pass, the hand is usually abandoned and deal passes to the left. But some players play a hand of competitive misere in no trump with whoever takes most tricks paying one unit to the other.

Proposal and acceptance is the lowest bid. Some solo players do not recognize it, but it can add to the enjoyment of a game. If a player thinks his hand could probably take four tricks, he calls 'propose'. A player with a similar hand may call 'accept' as long as no one else has bid solo or higher and the two form a partnership contracted to take eight tricks. Partners do not have to sit facing each other. Either the proposer or accepter should have some trump strength and lead them as soon as possible. If the proposal and acceptance was ill-advised, the opposition will be quick to spot any reluctance to lead trumps and grasp the advantage.

If a bid of solo stands, the bidder must take at least five tricks in the preferred trump suit. A good solo hand has length and/or strength in trump with a short, strong side suit and a void or singleton which gives the opportunity to use a low trump on an appropriate lead.

Players playing misere or spread misere must avoid taking any tricks, playing in no trump. As soon the caller makes a trick, the game stops and he pays up. Playing Spread Misere, the caller lays his cards face up on the table *after* the first trick has been played. Players should not be tempted to call either just because they have a poor hand. A good misere hand should have low ranking cards and a void. A hand with a long suit to ace, king can still be a good misere hand as long as there are several low cards in the long suit that can be played safely. The high cards can be discarded when a player leads the suit in which the caller is void.

Playing abundance, the caller must win at least nine tricks in a suit of his own choosing which he announces when the first trick is about to be played. The same minimum nine tricks must be taken by a player whose call of royal abundance stands, playing in the preferred trump suit. To call either, it is necessary to have length and strength in trumps, a good, long side suit and a void (two voids is better). Assess the hand by identifying definite losers: more than four and a call of either nine-trick abundances is ill advised.

The following hand stands a good chance of making abundance:

S – H A, K, Q, J, 10, 9   C 10, 8, 7, 5, 4, 2   D A

but not with hearts as the trump suit! If it was, there are too many club losers. But if the hand is played with clubs as trumps, the player can use them to flush out the four trump honours using the extra ones to ruff a spade lead and, after one round of diamonds, to ruff a diamond lead. With trumps out of the way, the caller's hearts winners are all established, giving him his nine tricks. He should, depending on how the other cards are distributed, make two trumps tricks, one diamond trick and six heart tricks.

Players must decide in advance the rules for declared abundance in which the caller has the privilege of leading. It is usually played in no trump, but some players allow a call of declared abundance in a specified suit which outranks a call of ordinary declared abundance but which in turn is outranked by a call of declared abundance in the preferred trump suit. Such a circumstance will happen only rarely, but it is best to decide in advance should it occur.

Rounds of declared abundance are rarely played out. The caller has to be quite certain that he is going to take all thirteen tricks. If he can see any way in which his call can be defeated, there is no point in calling it, as if it did go down it would cost him twenty-four units – eight to each player. His cards are laid down, but if a player can see a way of playing that can defeat it, the hand must be played.

QUINTO

Quinto is a deceptively simple game invented around the turn of the century by Angelo 'Professor Hoffman' Lewis. The game is played by four players in partnership, players facing each other across the table forming a partnership. Each player is dealt twelve cards from a 52-card pack into which a joker has been shuffled. The last five cards are the *cachette*.

Points are scored for each trick and for quints (see below).

Game is 250 points. Rubber is the best of three games, the winning partnership being awarded a bonus of 100 points.

After the *cachette* has been laid aside, but before a card is led, each player in turn can double the value of a trick. An opponent's double can be redoubled. Tricks are normally worth five points: a doubled trick is worth ten points: a redoubled trick scores twenty points. Doubling and redoubling affects the value of the trick, not of the quints. Tricks are scored at the end of each round: quints are scored when they are taken.

A quint is the joker, a five, and two cards that add up to five, i.e. an ace and a four of the same suit or a three and a two. A trick can contain more than one quint. If a side makes game as a result of winning a trick containing a quint, the rest of the hand is not played out.

Quints are valued as follows:

The joker (quint royal): 25

A quint in hearts: 20

A quint in diamonds: 15

A quint in clubs: 10

A quint in spades: 5

The joker has no trick taking value. It can be played *at any time*, out of suit, so it is best played when a partner has played a card that has already won the trick as it is quint royal and will score an immediate twenty-five points for that partnership.

Trump for each round is determined by the first card led. If a player is forced to lead the joker, the second card led determines the trump suit.

Players must follow suit. If they can't they discard or trump. And it is the trumping system that adds to the fun of the game. The lowest trump suit is spades, followed by clubs, then diamonds and hearts. So, on a spade lead, a player unable to follow is bound to trump it by playing any card from his hand apart from the joker. Diamonds trump any club or spade card, and hearts trump the other three suits.

At the end of the last round, the winning pair take the *cachette* and score any quints in it. The *cachette* also counts as a trick and is scored accordingly.

FALL OUT

Expose the top card of a 52-card pack to decide trump and then deal: four cards each if there are four players, five cards to each player if there are five players and six if there are six in the game.

Place the stock, face down in the centre of the table.

The player on the left of the dealer leads to the first trick. Thereafter, the winner of each trick leads to the next one. If players are unable to follow suit, they can trump or discard.

The winner of each trick takes the top card from the stock into his hand without exposing it to the other players.

Players drop out when they have run out of cards: the winner is the last player left in the game.

Fall Out can be played for cash when players put money into the pot and add to it each time they lose a trick. The winner takes all the money in the pot at the end of the game. It is less expensive to play for points. The first player to drop out scores one point: the second two and so on. First to break an agreed barrier wins. If two players reach the winning score on the same hand, the player who has scored fewer ones (or twos if they have both been first to drop out of the same number of games) is declared winner.

AUCTION PITCH

This is a game for four players who are each dealt six cards. Players take it in turns, starting with the player on the dealer's left, to bid the number of points they will take, scoring as follows:

High: one point for winning a trick with the highest trump card in play.

Low: one point for taking a trick with the lowest trump in play.

Jack: one point for taking a trick with the jack of trump if in play.

Game: one point for taking the most points in a round, scoring four for an ace, three for a king, two for a jack and ten for a ten.

Players can either pass or bid for at least two points. Each bid must be for more than the preceding one, except for the dealer who can bid the same as the previously highest bid. But if a player has bid four points, 'Smudge', the dealer cannot take the declaration.

The player who makes the highest bid is 'the maker'. The card he leads or 'pitches' determines trump.

Only if a player is unable to follow suit, can he trump or discard. The winner of a trick leads to the next.

Players record their own scores, as above. If the maker fails to make his contract, he reduces his score by the full amount of his declaration. This can result in his having a negative score, in which case he encircles it and is said to be in a hole.

The winner is the first player to reach seven. If two players reach that score in the same deal and one of them is the maker, he wins.

A player who successfully smudges wins the game outright unless he was in a hole when he smudged, when he only scores four points.

CANCELLATION HEARTS

This is a variation of Black Lady for six or more players.

Shuffle two packs of cards together: deal each player the same number of cards, and put the remainder in the widow.

Players	Cards dealt to each player	Cards in the widow
6	17	2
7	14	6
8	13	–
9	11	5
10	10	4

After the exchanges have been made, the player on the dealer's left leads. Some players have a rule that whoever wins the first trick, has the option of taking the widow, keeping as many cards as he wants from it and discarding an equal number.

Play is the same as for Black Lady (see page 68), the difference being that when two identical cards are played on a trick they cancel each other, ranking as zero and unable to take the trick. If for example a six is led and all the other cards played are higher but paired, they cancel each other leaving the six as the winning card.

If all cards played in a trick are cancelled, they remain on the table and go to the winner of the next trick.

Players are penalized one point for each heart card they take, and thirteen points for either of the Black Ladies.

GAMBLING GAMES

Card games played for money range from simple ones such as Newmarket where the stakes are rarely more than a few pence to much more complex games such as poker which can be played for small stakes or vast fortunes. Some games can be played just for fun or for cash. Be warned! What sounds like small stakes can mount up. A harmless invitation to play bridge for 'a small bit on the side' can result in temporary financial ruin as one university undergraduate found out to his cost. Having cashed his grant cheque (which wasn't very large) he drifted into the Student's Union where he was asked to 'make up a four' The stakes, a penny a hundred, sounded insignificant but several disastrous rubbers later he realized that his spending money for the entire term had been lost! A providential loan was soon repaid after a few good hands in a subsequent poker school. He was one of the lucky ones.

There is no doubt that playing for money does add an extra edge to a game but if you have to ask what the maximum stake is you probably can't afford the minimum and it's one of those annoying laws that you never (or at least very rarely) win when you need the money.

RED DOG

This is one of the simplest of all gambling games. Everyone puts an agreed number of units into the pot before being dealt five cards (four if there are more than nine players). The dealer places the stock in front of him. The player on his left looks at his hand and then bets anything from one unit to the entire pot that he has a higher card of the same suit as the top card on the stock. The dealer turns over the top card (aces are high). If the player can show a higher card of the same suit he is paid the amount equal to his stake from the pot. If he loses, his stake is added to the pot. Before the next player goes, the first player's cards and the card he bet against are put at the bottom of the pile after having been shown to the other players.

NAPOLEON

Three is the minimum number of players for this game which can be played by up to seven players. The game is addictive. Once it starts players have time for little else as passengers on a flight to a small Scottish airport can testify. The plane landed and was flagged into position: but nobody turned up to push the aircraft steps into position. Airline ground staff couldn't do it: not their job. The airport ground staff who could be found couldn't do it: not their job. For about three-quarters of an hour passengers and crew fumed inside the cabin, while less than 100 yards away in the bowels of the airport building the two duty drivers and three baggage handlers were engrossed in a cut-throat game of Napoleon.

Players are dealt five cards each from a 52-card pack. In some schools players are dealt their hands five cards at once, rather than having their cards dealt to them one at a time.

Players add one unit to the pot before each deal.

Once players have assessed their hands, they take it in turn to declare how many tricks they are going to take. The player on the dealer's left is first to bid. The next to go must bid a higher number of tricks or pass. Players bid once each. Whoever makes the highest bid plays against all the others. His lead card indicates trumps for that round.

Anyone who bids to take all five tricks is said to be going Napoleon, hence the name of the game.

If everyone passes, the cards are thrown in and a new deal is made by the person on the original dealer's left.

The usual rules apply: aces are high: players must follow suit.

Payment is made as follows:

Contract	Declarer wins	Declarer loses and pays
Two	2 units from each player	2 units to each player
Three	3 units from each player	3 units to each player
Four	4 units from each player	4 units to each player
Nap	10 units from each player	5 units to each player

There are no rewards for making overtricks. If there are any undertricks the contract has been defeated and the declarer pays out.

Players can also contract to lose all tricks in no trumps. This is known as 'misere' and ranks above a bid of three, but below a bid of four and pays or loses three units to each player.

If a contract goes down, the money in the pool stays where it is, and players add another unit to it before the next round is dealt. A player who makes his contract scoops the pool.

Napoleon was, of course, defeated by Wellington at the Battle of Waterloo. And a bid of Wellington outranks a Napoleon. This is a contract to win all five tricks at double stakes, winning twenty units from each player if successful, and paying ten if defeated.

Wellington himself can be outranked by a bid of Blucher (Blucher was a Prussian field marshal whose army arrived to support Wellington at a critical time during the Battle of Waterloo).

Blucher pays triple stakes for a five-trick contract. If the bidder makes it he receives thirty units: if not, he pays fifteen to the others.

There are two variations played in some schools.

In Peep Nap, the player who has the contract can look at the top card in the stock: if he wants it, he can swap it for any card in his hand.

In Purchase Nap, players can add one unit to the pool for the privilege of looking at the top card in the stock before the bid. A player who has paid to do this can, if he becomes declarer, swap the card for any one in his hand.

Good Nap players are skilled at remembering what cards have been played in previous rounds so that when they look at their hand, they have a fair idea (it can never be 100 per cent accurate) what cards have been distributed in the deal and what cards remain in the stock.

The odds on particular cards being in the stock or having been dealt vary according to the number of players. For example, if there are four players in a school and one of them is dealt three cards in a suit which he considers bidding on, the odds against any other player having three or more cards in that suit are just over 16 to 1.

NEWMARKET

Fix the stakes before starting to play this enjoyable game of chance. Most schools decide on a smallish pot and a fixed stake for the boodle cards – as high or as low as they can afford.

Deal to each player the same number of cards from a 52-card pack to each player. The remaining cards are the dummy or widow and are placed face down on the table.

Number of players	Cards in each hand	Cards in the widow
3	13	13
4	10	12
5	8	12
6	7	10
7	6	10
8	5	12

You also need the ace, king, queen and knave from another pack, all of different suits. These are the horses running at Newmarket, more properly called the boodle cards – the ones on which players put their stakes.

Before players look at their hands, they put their money into the pool and place their stakes on the boodle cards. They must back at least one 'horse'. They can wager the fixed stake on all four if they so wish. They are hoping that the card or cards they back will be in their hand, and that they will get the chance to play them.

After everyone has looked at their hands, the dealer auctions the dummy hand provided he doesn't want it himself. In some schools, the dealer keeps the money paid for it, in others, the dealer gets it for nothing, but whoever buys it puts the money paid for it into the pot. When a player buys the dummy, his original hand is put face down on the table and becomes the new dummy. If the dealer doesn't want the dummy and no one wants to buy it, it stays where it is.

The player on the dealer's left starts the game by playing the lowest card he holds in whatever suit he wants, placing it face up on the table in front of him. Whoever has the next card in sequence does the same. And so on until the run comes to stop because the next card in sequence must be in dummy (or has been played before as the first card in a sequence).

Whoever played the last card starts a new sequence playing the lowest card in whatever suit he wants.

Anyone who plays a card that matches one of the boodle cards collects all the money staked on it.

The first player to get rid of all his cards, scoops the kitty. Unclaimed wagers remain on the boodle cards for the next round.

Newmarket is also known as Boodle, after the cards: and in the United States it is known as Saratoga – after one of America's famous race courses.

NEWMARKET

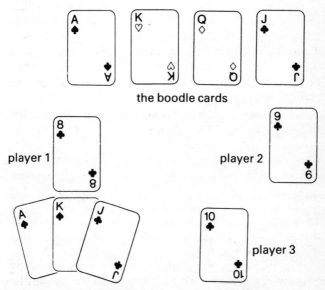

the boodle cards

player 1

player 2

player 3

Player 1 has led the eight of clubs. Player 2 has the nine and plays it, and player 3 plays the ten. Player 1 can now play the jack of clubs and claim the money staked on that boodle card. If no one has the queen, he can play his king of spades and then the ace to pick up the money staked on the ace.

DRAW POKER

In Draw Poker, five cards are dealt to the players from a 52-card pack. (In some games the jokers are left in and are floating cards having whatever value the holder wishes them to have.)

The sequence of winning hands is as follows:

1) Straight flush – five consecutive cards of the same suit.

2) Four of a kind – the four cards of equal pip value.

3) Full house – three cards of equal pip value (a prial) and a pair of equal pip value.

4) Flush – five cards of the same suit.

5) A run – five consecutive cards of different suits.

6) Three of a kind – a prial.

7) Two pairs – two sets of cards of equal pip value.

8) One pair.

9) No pair.

If two players have the same hand, the highest card determines the winner: For example, if two players have a straight flush, the one with the highest top card wins. The highest straight flush is a royal one, ace, king, queen, jack and ten. If two players have four of a kind, the one with the highest cards wins. The pip value of the prial in a full house determines the winner (three queens and two twos beats three jacks and two aces). Aces are high except in the case of the lowest run – ace, two, three, four, five,

Before each deal (the deal passes clockwise round the table) players put their ante into the pot – usually a quarter of the minimum stake. Five cards are then dealt one at a time to each player. The player on the dealer's left starts. If he thinks his hand has absolutely no potential he can throw it in.

If he wants to stay in the game he puts in the minimum stake or double it. The next player has the choice of throwing his hand in, or staying in the game by matching the first player's stake or raising it. Each player has either to equal or increase the previous stake. Staking continues until no player left in raises, when all players remaining in the game will have an equal stake in the pot. A player who throws in his hand forfeits his ante and any money he may have staked.

Once staking has finished, the players can exchange cards in their hands for fresh ones from the pack. They can ask for complete new hands if they wish, but it is rare for players to ask for more than three new cards as a pair is usually the minimum necessary to stay in.

Once everyone has their new cards the second round of staking begins with the player who first staked. Players can stay in the game keeping the stake the same – checking – or by raising it. As soon as one player raises the stake, everyone else must put in a stake equal to the raise (calling) or raise it again. A player who has checked may call but not raise.

Betting continues until all the players except one have thrown their hands in. In this case, the winner takes all the money in the pot without showing his cards. When there has been a complete round of calling (no players raising the stake) or when a maximum stake has been reached, there is a showdown when the player who made the last raise shows his hand: the other player or players may concede without revealing their cards: in poker you only reveal your cards if you are claiming the pot.

Good poker playing depends on bluff and skill: bluff, to persuade other players that you have a better hand than you have, hoping to convince them to throw in their hands without calling yours; skill, to assess the probabilities of improving a hand, to assess what other players hold, to assess whether the stake required to stay in a game is worth the risk in relation to the pot.

Good poker players know what the odds are of improving whatever they hold in their hand. For example, if they hold a prial and draw two cards, the odds against drawing a pair to make a full house are around 15-1: the odds against drawing the card necessary to get four of a kind are roughly 22-1. But if you hold four cards of the same suit and ask for one new card, there's just more than a 4-1 chance that it will complete the flush.

People who win at poker throw in poor hands, knowing that there is no second prize; it's winner takes all. They neither throw good money after bad, nor do they over-react by raising rashly when they get a good hand. They don't bluff too often, but just enough to keep other players guessing.

DRAW POKER

Player 1 has little chance of improving his hand, so he should stack it.

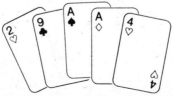

Player 2 draws three new cards, discarding the 2H, 9C and 4H.

Player 3 keeps his two sixes and the queen and draws two new cards.

   Player 4 could keep his twos and draw three new cards but as both players left in have drawn two and three cards, they probably held at least a pair as well. He decides to take a risk, discards the 2D and takes one new card.

Hands are now:

player 2

The three new cards have done nothing to improve the hand.

player 4

The discard of the two diamonds has paid off: the hand is now a spade flush.

player 3

A dramatic improvement: a full house – sixes over queens.

The player with the pair of aces would probably drop out after a round or two leaving the players with the full house and the flush to fight it out. When either player stops raising, the player who made the last rise shows his cards. If the player with the flush was to expose his hand, the player with the full house would show his cards to claim the pot. If the player with the full house was the one to show his cards first, the other player would concede by giving his cards to the dealer who puts them unseen at the bottom of the pack.

PONTOON

The word 'pontoon' is a corruption of the French *vingt-et-un*. The aim of the game is to collect cards with a total pip value of up to twenty-one, and not beyond.

The game which was popular with British soldiers and sailors during the Second World War has never acquired the chic of baccarat or chemin de fer although it demands a high degree of skill as well as that essential element in winning at cards – luck.

Cut a 52-card pack to decide dealer, who in pontoon is also the banker. The cards from two to ten carry their pip value. Court cards are worth ten, and aces either one or eleven, whichever the holders wish. The banker plays each player in turn. To start he deals one card to each player before dealing one to himself. He doesn't look at his own card.

The aim of the game is to build up a hand with a maximum pip value of twenty-one. Beyond this a player is 'burst' – out of the game. Players look at their first card and stake according to its potential. A ten or an ace is worth a good stake: so are low cards such as twos or threes: mid-value cards are more difficult to assess.

When all the stakes have been placed, the banker deals second cards to each person, including himself, again not looking at his own hand. The first player (the one on the dealer's left) now plays his hand. He may decide to stick on what he has, or to 'twist' in which case the banker turns up the top card of the pack and gives it to the player. Players can twist a maximum of three times, but must declare as soon as the pip value of his hand adds up to more than twenty-one. Players can also 'buy' cards from the banker, in which case they are given to the player face down. They cannot buy cards for more than they have originally staked. If the pip value of a hand exceeds twenty-one, all the money that player has staked including the money he has paid for bought cards, is forfeit to the bank.

A player who is dealt two cards of equal value can 'split'. His two cards become the first cards of two separate hands. The banker deals him two more cards, one for each base card, and the player now plays both his hands against the banker, one at a time.

If a player's first two cards add up to fourteen, he can ask the banker for new cards. The first is dealt face down: the second is dealt open.

When the first player either sticks or declares himself burst, the second player now bets his hand against the banker. And so on until the banker has played everyone in turn. He now turns up his hand, either sticking or twisting to try to get his score as close to twenty-one as possible. When he sticks, everyone declares their hands. All hands equal to or of lesser pip score than the banker's are beaten by the banker who collects all the money staked on them. Players who have a higher pip count than the banker are paid whatever they have staked by him.

Five card tricks (hands with five cards which add up to less than twenty-one) are paid at 3 – 1. Pontoons – a hand made up of two cards adding up to exactly twenty-one (i.e. an ace and a court card or ten – are paid at 2 – 1. If the banker and another player both have a five-card trick, the winning hand is the one with the lower pip count. If the banker has a five-card trick the others have to pay him three times their stake: if he has a pontoon, they pay him twice their stake.

A pontoon composed of an ace/king beats an ace/queen, which is higher than an ace/knave which, in turn beats an ace/ten.

The highest hand of all is three sevens. The banker pays the holder of such a hand at 4 – 1: and if the banker turns up three sevens, he collects four times the money staked from each player. A player who declares a pontoon is offered the bank. If he doesn't want it, he can sell it to another player.